WATERFALLS OF THE WORLD

1974 1st

WATERFALLS

OF THE

WORLD

A PICTORIAL SURVEY

RITA M. BARTON BA FRGS

D. BRADFORD BARTON LIMITED

Frontispiece: **Gokak Falls, India**   One of the finest spectacles in Asia are the 170' high Gokak Falls in Mysore. Often obscured by spray after the onset of the monsoon, they are seen here at relatively low water. Overlooking the river at their base and utilising the tremendous power available, are the Gokak Cotton Mills.

Rhine Falls, Schaffhausen, on the border between Switzerland and West Germany.

introduction

Every year, millions of people from all far corners of the earth visit Niagara and depart with the satisfaction of having seen—or so they believe—the greatest of the world's waterfalls. Of the mighty Sete Quedas, of Rua Cana, Cauvery, Kaieteur and the Khon Cataracts, of Gullfoss and Gersoppa, Iguaçu, Paulo Affonso, Aughrabies or the Angel Falls, they know nothing. Indeed, other than Niagara, the Victoria Falls on Africa's Zambesi is the only other giant waterfall generally well known.

With the expansion of world tourism, the names of this élite, at present so unfamiliar, will become reality for an increasing number of people. Already the more affluent or intrepid have begun an invasion of the fastnesses where many of these unknown mammoths are to be found. For instance, in South America, where a large proportion of them is located, it is now possible to fly out to the otherwise inaccessible Angel Falls, highest in the world, yet discovered only 40 years ago; to visit the colossus, Iguaçu, in the Brazilian jungle; and in a small sea-plane to experience the thrill of lift-off from the rim of Guyana's lonely and lofty Kaieteur. The continent's other titans, Sete Quedas and Paulo Affonso, together with further spectacular falls, such as the Brazilian Urubupunga, Colombia's Tequendama and and those on the Laja River in Chile, still await popular discovery. In Africa, the same trend is evident. The number of visitors to Victoria Falls mounts rapidly each year that passes, while the impressive Nile waterfalls of Tisisat in Ethiopia and Uganda's Kabalega are beginning to attract similar attention. As in South America, however, a number of the continent's finest falls lie in areas which are inhospitable or remote—Rua Cana and the savage Aughrabies Falls in the south-western desert, for instance, and Maletsunyane, terror of the Bantus, on the roof-top of Africa, in Lesotho. Of the great falls of Asia even less is known; in Laos and India, three monsoon-fed mammoths lie virtually undiscovered by the world at large—the Mekong's Khon Cataracts, for sheer volume second in the world only to Sete Quedas; in Mysore the Cauvery Falls, close rival to both the foregoing, and nearby Gersoppa, provider of light and power for a large part of peninsular India. Finally, in Australasia, where great waterfalls are few, there are the lofty Sutherland Falls. At the end of the earth, in the *ultima Thule* of New Zealand's 'Fiordland', they languish quite forgotten, for all their height and beauty, which only the Angel Falls and California's Yosemite are known to exceed.

The increasing affluence and mobility of Europeans and North Americans which are gradually extending their horizons to include these select few of the waterfalls of the world have already familiarised them with countless others, smaller but much more accessible. Fifty years ago, before the advent of cheap and rapid transport, even these falls were known only to the relative few. There come to mind, primarily, the multitudes of Swiss waterfalls, best known and best loved of all, among them the Rheinfall, Reichenbach, Pissvache and Staubbach. Then there are the rather less familiar Scandinavian giants: Iceland's Dettifoss, Gullfoss and Godafoss; Stora Sjöfallet and Harsprånget in Sweden, and the many beautiful examples along Norway's fjord coast. In North America, apart from Niagara and the remote Churchill Falls of Labrador, the finest waterfalls lie primarily in the great vacation areas of the Rockies: the much visited Yosemite, second highest in the world, together with the other impressive falls of Yosemite National Park; the falls of the Yellowstone River and those on the Columbia-Snake River complex in Washington and Oregon, as well as other magnificent examples in the Cascade and Coast Ranges of the northern Rockies.

What is it about these waterfalls, large or small, which fascinates? The three superlatives attract simply because they are record breakers: Angel Falls, the highest, interminable, dropping from the clouds; the broadest, Khon Cataracts, a white tumult wide as the world; and Sete Quedas, in summer spate one full-throated, terrifying roar, most powerful of them all. In their presence one is at first mesmerised, subject to unfamiliar emotions compounded of wonder and of fear. They are feelings which in the more primitive mind equate with a misdirected reverence or superstition, in the most sensitive with artistic inspiration. At one extreme there comes to mind, for instance, the Barotse 'Spirit' of Victoria Falls, or the mythical deities of Iceland's Godafoss, as well as Aughrabies' all-consuming and monstrous 'Groote Slang'; and at the other, Wordsworth's 'sky-born' Staubbach; the torrent of the Gasteiner Ache, its music perpetuated in a Schubert symphony, or Turner's falls in Switzerland, the Reichenbach and Rheinfall.

But there are also, on closer acquaintance, more tranquil pleasures, arising out of leisurely contemplation of the movement and texture of falling water, which together create a loveliness of which one never tires. It is a beauty at once both transient and reassuringly immutable. Moment by passing moment, season by season, the leaping river changes its voice, its mood, its aspect, in sensitive response to the varying elements around it—sunlight or scudding shadow; wind and storm; darkness; or the cold clasp of winter—never quite the same yet, a lifetime later, little changed at all. Moreover, in addition to the intrinsic beauty of waterfalls themselves, the physical and mental excitements that they arouse, the scenes of sparkling animation which they create, and their refreshing cool in the heat and dust of day, there are other, casual enhancements which often take the onlooker by surprise. There are those dark, mysterious pools and caverns, foils to the water's foaming whiteness, which lie below and behind the falls; and in contrast to both, the lively colour of the swiftly sliding river upon the brink; sunny turquoise or a cold and glacial grey; green and glassy like Niagara perhaps; silt-stained to amber, orange, russet red; or darkly sombre like the Potaro and Laja of South America. There are, too, the colonies of wild birds which so frequently make the falls their home as well as the relative luxuriance of vegetation which the broken water engenders, whether it is the intimate beauty of hidden moss and fern or the emerald exuberance of jungle growth, glittering and dripping beneath a drenching rain of spray. Then again, and most beautiful of all perhaps, there are those iridiscent rainbows which, on sunny days, arch and glance within the drifting spray, as well as the paler, lunar arcs that are more rarely seen, finest of all those of Victoria Falls, shimmering like spectres in the African night.

It is ironic that frequently the very attribute which makes a waterfall remarkable renders it difficult to photograph. Indeed, until the days of the aeroplane, many of the higher or wider falls, in addition to those situated in difficult terrain, were impossible to record in their entirety, if at all. As this volume demonstrates, only the airborne camera can do full justice to such photogenic giants as Yosemite; Africa's Rua Cana, Aughrabies or Maletsunyane; the Angel Falls; or Niagara and Victoria, while some important examples— the Tamarind Falls of Mauritius, for instance—elude even this approach. Moreover, many of the most powerful waterfalls, such as Gersoppa in Mysore, are so obscured by spray when in spate that they can only be photographed other than in the wet season, while problems of a more technical nature present themselves to the photographer working under gloomy, sub-arctic skies or before the blinding glitter of tropical falls set in a uniformly dense and dark green jungle.

During this century, numerous waterfalls—in particular those of exceptional height or volume—have been changed beyond all recognition by their utilisation for irrigation purposes or for the generation of hydro-electric power. Some of them, almost entirely re-channelled, have virtually vanished from the scene. Norway's most beautiful Rjukanfoss, ravished long ago, is one; others, sadly depleted or else spoiled by the proximity of pipelines and power stations, serve only as a reminder of their former glory. As man's demands upon his environment increase, more and more of the world's rivers and their waterfalls are being harnessed in this way, often to their full capacity. The Waikato in New Zealand, Sweden's Lule and the Snake River of America are each yoked, for instance, not once but many times, and it is probably only a matter of years before such remote beauties as Iceland's Godafoss are eventually tamed for the benefit of mankind. In the meantime, a lesson has been learned in some instances: by the Royal Board of Waterfalls in Sweden, for example, where on 'Waterfall Days' the Göta River is loosed once again down the Trollhättan Falls; in the case of the Barron Falls in Queensland which, on occasion, for the benefit of tourists, are allowed briefly to regain their full and former splendour; and in the weekend beauty of Italy's Cascata delle Marmore, temporarily released from the bonds of its workaday toil. To see these waterfalls spring to full life again is to see the landscape revivified—a timely reminder of what man stands to lose on one hand as he gains upon the other.

ACKNOWLEDGEMENTS

The author and publishers thank the following for the loan of photographs:
Agent General for Tasmania, London Aktieselkabet Tyssefaldene, Tyssedal, Norway Austrian State Tourist Department, Vienna Brazilian Embassy, London British Columbia Department of Travel Industry, Victoria Bruce Moss, Ontario, Canada Centro de Informacao e Turismo de Angola, Luanda Director General of Tourist Services, Brisbane, Queensland Don Stephens & Associates, Lindisfarne, Tasmania Ecuador Embassy, London Embassy of Finland, London French Government Tourist Office, London Gokak Mills Ltd, Mysore Government of the Province of Alberta Guyana High Commission, London Hawaii Visitors Bureau, Honolulu High Commissioner for New Zealand, London Idaho Department of Commerce & Development Italian State Tourist Office, London Jamaica Tourist Board, Kingston Laotian Embassy, London Loftleidir (Icelandic Airlines), Reykjavik Malawi Ministry of Information, Blantyre Mauritius High Commission, London Montana Highway Commission Mysore Government Department of Industry & Tourism Newfoundland & Labrador Tourist Development Office, St. Johns New South Wales Department of Tourism, Sydney New York State Department of Commerce North Central State Ministry of Information, Nigeria Norway Travel Association, Oslo Norwegian State Railways, Oslo Norwegian Water Resources & Electricity Board, Oslo Ontario Ministry of Industry & Tourism Oregon State Highways Department Papua New Guinea Department of Information, Port Moresby Philippines Tour & Travel Association, Manila Quebec Department of Tourism Rhodesia National Tourist Board, Salisbury Royal Swedish Embassy, London Satour (South African Tourist Corporation), Pretoria Swiss National Tourist Office, Zurich The Royal Geographical Society, London Trinidad & Tobago Tourist Board, Port of Spain Turkish Embassy, London Uganda Ministry of Tourism, Kampala U.S. Department of the Interior, National Park Service Washington State Tourist Promotion Division Wyoming Travel Commission Yugoslav National Tourist Office, London Zambia National Tourist Office, Lusaka

Stora Sjöfallet, Sweden Well within the Arctic Circle, the innumerable lakes and rivers of Lappland lie frozen in a waste of win darkness for many months of the year. With the late spring thaw, the meltwaters are released in flood, coursing down in tumult to t icy Baltic two hundred miles to the east. The falls of Stora Sjöfallet, seen here, are a complex of rapids and two waterfalls forming pa of the descent of the Lule River.

EUROPE

Harsprånget Falls, Sweden Continuing the descent of its great water staircase to the sea after leaving Stora Sjöfallet, the Lule River negotiates six cataracts, interrupted in their midst by the Porjus Falls, before reaching the famous Harsprånget Falls. These numerous waterfalls, together with others which lie farther downstream, represent Sweden's greatest reserves of hydro-electric power and several, including Harsprånget, have been utilised for this purpose. Formerly one of Europe's most magnificent falls, the latter derives its name from the belief that a hare could spring across the narrow gorge through which the river pours; others hold that it was the graceful ice arch, formed from the freezing winter mists above the fall, which afforded the wild creature an easy crossing.

10

Trollhättan Falls, Sweden Far from the desolate grandeur of Sweden's Norrland lakes lie the Trollhättan Falls which, together with Alvkarleby Falls on the Dalä River, form the principal source of hydro-electric power in the south. The former, much depleted on this account, lie on the Göta River, outlet of the hundred mile-long Lake Vanern. However, if the lake is sufficiently high on 'Waterfall Days'— Sundays and summer festivals—water is released over the mile-long run of the falls and crowds gather to enjoy their brief renaissance.

Handöl Falls, Sweden
On its journey from the
Sylarna mountain area in
central Sweden's Jämt-
land, the Handölan River
descends in a succession
of rocky steps over a
distance of 390′. These
are the 195′ high Handöl
Falls, situated near the
village of Enafors, and
within a short distance of
the Norwegian border.

Krimml Falls, Austria
Plunging in clouds of
sunlit spray through
mountain forest, resin-
scented in the summer
warmth, are the melt-
waters of the Krimml
glacier. Originating in the
snowy Hohe Tauern
Range within a few miles
of the Italian frontier,
they drop here some
1400′ in three giant
cascades, the highest of
which is 460′. Down-
stream, the river then
enters the Saltzach,
tributary of the Inn,
which in turn joins the
Danube and so to the
Black Sea through
Salzburg and Vienna.

Bad Gastein Falls, Austria Also rising in the Hohe Tauern Range on the border between the Austrian provinces of Salzburg and Carinthia, the Gasteiner Ache, in a parallel valley to the Krimmler Ache, descends steeply to join the Saltzach. At Bad Gastein the river, plunging as a torrent through narrow ravines from the upper levels of the valley, forms a gigantic waterfall which divides the spa into two parts. Its total length is nearly 4000′, its drop 360′. Inspired by this waterfall, Schubert composed his 'Gastein Symphony'.

Saut du Doubs, France
Rising in the beautiful
mountain scenery of the
limestone Jura, the River
Doubs virtually encircles
this massif as it journeys
to join the Saône, which
then meets the Rhône at
Lyon, and so continues
to the Mediterranean. In
its mountain course,
not far from Berne on the
Swiss plateau below, the
young Doubs forms the
boundary between
France and Switzerland.
It is here that the Saut
du Doubs occurs.
Leaving the last of five
rock-bound lakes strung
out in line along its
valley, the river, fed by
the wet west wind known
there tersely as 'le vent',
makes a spectacular
90′ free fall into a deep
gorge below.

Godafoss, Iceland Godafoss, 'The Fall of the Gods', is situated between Akureyri and Lake Myvatn in northern Iceland. Reached only by a rudimentary road, it is an integral part of a primeval and heroic landscape which lies alternately beneath the flickering Northern Lights of the interminable Arctic winter and the mysterious illumination of a summer Midnight Sun. Although of no great height the fall, which plunges some 30′ into the River Skjalfandafljot, is impressive by virtue of its immense strength and power.

Gullfoss, Iceland Laden with fine glacial débris, the milk-like waters of the ice-cold Hvita (or White) River journey only eighty miles from the everlasting snows of Iceland's mountainous interior before reaching the southern coast. Yet this short river boasts one of Europe's most splendid waterfalls, Gullfoss, its teeming waters enhanced by the dark volcanic rock through which it pours, its tumult and turmoil by the silence and stillness of desolate surroundings. 'Gullfoss, 'The Golden Waterfall', comprises two main falls which lie at right angles to each other; an upper series of foaming, stepped cascades and, below, the main fall where on sunny days, rainbows shimmer in the rising spray.

Krka Falls, Yugoslavia
Rising in the massive Dinaric Alps of Yugoslavia, the Krka River carves its way westwards through the mountains to enter the island-studded Adriatic at the ancient port of Sibenik. Not far from its mouth the Krka, dividing and re-uniting in a wealth of waterfalls, descends through fragrant Mediterranean vegetation to the lovely Lake Prukljansko downstream.

Jacje Falls, Yugoslavia The hill town of Jacje in Bosnia lies in wooded surroundings on the banks of the rivers Pliva and Vrbas. A particular attraction is the graceful 60′ high waterfall on the first-named river above which, tier upon tier, rise the steeply roofed houses of this once important medieval town.

Pliva watermills, Yugoslavia These quaint and diminutive watermills, stilted and propped as they are above the cascading Pliva River, are reminiscent almost of some prehistoric lake village. The dilapidated buildings, with their timber water-conduits and creaking wheels at least a century old, are indicative of a peasant economy slowly slipping away. They are clustered around a number of waterfalls which link two picturesque lakes in the vicinity of Jacje.

Plitvice Lakes, Yugoslavia In northern Yugoslavia there lies a vast limestone gorge enclosed by thickly wooded mountains which extend down to the shores of sixteen crystal-clear lakes, blue, emerald and pale green. Each of these lakes, within the gorge, is fed by numerous mountain brooklets and all are interconnected by countless cascades and a complex of waterfalls. In early summer, when the air is filled with bird-song and the sound of rushing waters, the Plitvice Lakes are singularly beautiful; in winter their loveliness takes on a different aspect.

Rhine Falls, Switzerland Rising in the high Alps not far from the Italian border, the Rhine, mightiest of Europe's rivers, is swelled by the perpetually thawing ice of numerous Swiss glaciers before reaching its great waterfall at Schaffhausen below Lake Constance. The river, here dividing Switzerland from West Germany, drops over a wide rim of resistant limestone about 60′ deep and, when in full spate during July, is an awe-inspiring spectacle. A huge limestone crag juts out into the river in the centre of the falls and close beneath this a cockleshell of a boat plies during the tourist months of summer, with predictable effects upon its crowded occupants.

Zweistufiger Fall, Switzerland A pastoral symphony heard by few, the musical waters of the remote Zweistufiger Fall in the Saas Tal, Valais, find their way from the icy southern ramparts of Switzerland northwards to join the infant Rhône at Visp.

Reichenbach Falls, Switzerland Not far from the popular resort of Interlaken lie the Reichenbach Falls on a tributary of the River Aare. Fed by snows below the giant peaks of the Bernese Alps, the Reichenbach stream cascades first over the lovely Rosenlauibad Fall before receiving icy waters issuing from the snout of the Rosenlaui glacier. Greatly increased in volume, its precipitous descent is continued into the Aare valley through a wooded ravine, dropping a distance in all of almost 2000′ over seven splendid waterfalls.

Staubbach, Switzerland Most eulogized of Switzerland's many falls is Wordsworth's 'sky-born waterfall', the Staubbach, near Interlaken. The Lauterbrunnen valley into which it plunges was gouged out by past glacial action to a depth of more than a thousand feet and over the precipitous side of this vast ravine the Pletschenbach stream plunges as if from the clouds. Of small volume, the descending water is lifted by the wind before it reaches the valley floor and is blown like a veil across the wet cliff face, to disperse in mist among the trees.

Biasca Fall, Switzerland One of numerous cascades on snow-fed rivers draining south from the cold Alpine passes to the warm levels of Lake Maggiore in Italian Switzerland, this waterfall at Biasca beneath the St. Gothard Pass spouts in full flood into the main valley below.

Cascata di Boffalora, Switzerland In a neighbouring valley to the Biasca Falls lies the Cascata di Boffalora, the waters of which find their way into the Moesa River and so southwards to enter Lake Maggiore in the sun-baked Alpine foothills.

24

Pissvache, Switzerland
Often described as one
of the loveliest of Swiss
waterfalls, the Pissvache
lies in Valais, the canton
of giant mountains.
Originating in a glacial
cirque on the flanks of
the great Dent du Midi,
the Salanfe River pours
in torrent to the Rhône,
not many miles from its
entrance ot Lake
Geneva. When the snows
melt in June, the
Pissvache is at its best,
the Salanfe emerging
from a narrow gorge to
slide two hundred feet
over a cliff of black slate
in a foam of white water.

Sarpsfoss, Norway   In a country where countless rivers have carved short, precipitous courses to the sea, the Glomma stands apart. Rising not far from the Norwegian Sea near Trondheim, it traverses some 350 miles—about one third of the length of the country—before entering Oslofjord near the capital. During this journey it gathers strength to become the mightiest of Europe's rivers where volume is concerned, in full flood exceeding that of the Victoria Falls on the Zambesi. Although only 65′ high, about one-fifth of the height of the latter, Sarpsfoss is a source of tremendous power and has been harnessed to provide electricity in this most densely populated region of Norway.

Vøringsfoss, Norway   One of the most wonderful sights in southern Norway, Vøringsfoss lies near Bergen above the head of the 105 mile-long Hardangerfjord. From the high fjelds, the Bjøreio River, tributary of the Eio, courses down in a series of cascades as far as a road bridge above the fall; thereafter, it plunges 500′ into the great ravine below, its spray and thunder rising up to the plateau edge. It is in this spray that annular rainbows can sometimes be seen, while in winter the fall is a breath-taking spectacle of glittering curtains, stalactites and pinnacles of ice. In the gorge below, a rough path can be seen leading up to the foot of the fall, where the best view is obtained.

Skjeggedalsfoss and Tyssestrengene Falls, Norway

The waterfalls Tyssestrengene (above) and Skjeggedalsfoss (below) lie within a short distance of each other in southern Norway, each dropping from an ice-scoured landscape of scree and snow, corries and bare rock ridges into the deep mountain lake called Ringdalsvatn. Skjeggedalsfoss, one of the greatest and most beautiful of Norwegian falls, descends a height of 1200' overall, while the twin Tyssestrengene Falls have a sheer drop of over 900' down a vertical cliff face. The Ringdalsvatn is drained at its lower end by the Tysso River into Sörfjord, which in turn opens into the well known Hardangerfjord. On leaving the lake, the natural course of the Tysso, now harnessed to provide power for the Tyssedal aluminium works, is over another waterfall, the 90' high Sjoarfoss. It was the damming of the Ringdalsvatn which caused the water level to rise and the two former waterfalls to be considerably reduced in height.

Låtefoss, Norway In an area rich in waterfalls—Skjeggedalsfoss and Tyssestrengene, for instance, as well as Jordalsfoss, Hildalsfoss and Eidefoss—lies the wonderful fall popularly referred to as Låtefoss. In fact, Låtefoss is really two waterfalls, Skarsfoss (right) and Låtefoss itself (left). Both spring from the same lake; both are about 1200′ long and 495′ high and together they enshroud their immediate surroundings with fine spray, a wonderful sight on a sunny day. The river is the Austdøla, which flows to join the Opo near Odda, and so enters Sörfjord, an inlet of Hardangerfjord.

Vettifoss, Norway Pouring from the savage Jotunheim Mountains, the Morkakoldedøla River hastens to join the River Utla on its way to Norway's magnificent Sognefjord. A fall of surpassing beauty, for 1000′ it streams downwards in a mare's tail of white foam, hidden from the world in a solitude of forest and rushing waters. In winter it is entrapped as a glittering ice column hung with countless stalactites.

Rojanefoss, Norway Some of the most magnificent scenery in Norway lies in the West Country of Vestlandet, south of the 125 mile-long Sognefjord. It is an area of high barren moors, lofty peaks rising above ice caps and their fringing glaciers, of cold, rushing rivers, waterfalls and forests of pine or spruce. On the brighter days of Spring, when the drizzle and mists of the west coast winter disperse and the snows are melting under a welcome sun, Norway's waterfalls like Rojanefoss, above Sognefjord near Flåm, spring to full life, streaming like white pennants against their sombre setting of rock and dark trees.

Syv Söstre, Norway   Like the mountain valleys of Switzerland, the fjords of Norway, deep and cliff-sided, were gouged out by ice. In the same way her waterfalls, like their Swiss counterparts, find their way to the glaciated valley floors—in Norway drowned by the sea—in vertical drops of great height. The well-known Syv Söstre or Seven Sisters—they number only four at low water—descend in this way into Geirangerfjord near Alesund. Of exquisite beauty, delicate and feminine, they fall and rest, fall and rest, like long and silken tresses upon the bare shoulders of the valley.

Vermafoss, Norway
Immediately north of
Geirangerfjord lies Romsdals-
fjord, into which the waters of
Vermafoss eventually find their
way. Seen from the opposite
side of the valley, the long,
cascading course of the river
is particularly beautiful.
Whiter than the melting snow
which feeds it, the water,
crossed by a number of
seemingly frail bridges, finds
its way through dense forest
of spruce and fir. Finally it
divides into three separate
falls before turning and making
its way to the sea.

Adamsfoss, Norway An awe-inspiring sight from the road northbound to Vardö and the Russian frontier, Adamsfoss lies in Finnmark, land of long twilights, the most remote and northerly region of Norway. Little but the endless drift-ice of the Arctic Ocean lies between the North Pole and the Laksefjord into which the falls plunge; as they lie in polar darkness for many months of the year, enjoyment of them is restricted to the rare visitor in the brief northern summer.

Cascata delle Marmore, Italy   In the heart of peninsular Italy, set among the beautiful mountains of rustic Umbria, lies the Cascata delle Marmore. One of the highest falls in Europe, it has the distinction of being an artificial creation of BC 272, when the Consul Curius Dentatus diverted the River Veline into the River Nera. The waters, which form a breathtaking spectacle when floodlit, are set free only on holidays and at weekends, then finding their way into the Tiber and so to Rome. At other times, they are harnessed for industrial purposes.

Pitsus Falls, Finland In a country where it is estimated there are some 60,000 lakes and that one tenth of the total area is water-covered, it is inevitable that there are innumerable waterfalls. The Pitsus Falls lie in Finnish Lappland near Enontakio, amid a wilderness of pine forests, raging rivers and barren fjells. This is an area most beautiful of all when, with the first onset of winter cold, comes the 'ruska,' that brilliant colouring of autumn foliage which blazes like forest fire during one brief week in September.

THE AMERICAS

Ram River Falls, Alberta, Canada   Although generally regarded as one of the 'Prairie Provinces' of Canada, a considerable portion of Alberta lies in the Rockies, where marvellous scenery has brought about the creation of several National Parks. Of the numerous waterfalls in this westernmost part of the Province, the Ram River Falls, situated where the river leaves dark spruce forests to plunge over the rim of a rocky amphitheatre, are particularly impressive.

Bow Falls, Alberta, Canada On the eastern slopes of the Rocky Mountain Divide, near the Kicking Horse Pass, lies the Banff National Park of Alberta. Here, near Banff itself and in a magnificent mountain setting, the Bow River, bound for Calgary and the South Saskatchewan River, tumbles in a cascade of snowy water over the falls which share its name.

Sunwaysta Falls, Alberta, Canada Some 200 miles north of the Kicking Horse Pass, where a tributary of the Athabasca River affords another of the three principal routes over the high Canadian Rockies —the Yellowhead Pass— lies the Jasper National Park. In this area of giant peaks, glaciers and waterfalls lie the Sunwaysta Falls, a torrent of white water set amid tall pines which clothe the mountain slopes below the snow line.

O'Hara Falls, British Columbia, Canada   Near the Kicking Horse Pass, on the western side of the great water-parting of the Canadian Rockies, lies Yoho National Park. Here the snowfields and glaciers of twenty-eight peaks over 10,000′ swell the waters of feeders to the great Columbia River, which winds its way to the Pacific coast in Washington. One of these tributaries is the Kicking Horse River that crosses the Park from east to west. It receives the waters of O'Hara Falls, which lie in magnificent mountaineering country above O'Hara Lake, well-known for its green translucency.

39

Takakkaw Falls, British Columbia, Canada
Dropping into forests of Lodgepole pine, blue fir and spruce, where elk, moose and deer roam freely, are the Takakkaw Falls of Yoho National Park. One of the most spectacular of Canada's waterfalls, they leap a sheer 1200′ from a hanging valley high above the level, glaciated valley of the Yoho River, tributary of the Kicking Horse River. Their waters are derived from the meltwaters of the Daly Glacier on the edge of the Waputik icefield.

Twin Falls, British Columbia, Canada Accentuating the sheer walls of the ice-scoured valley into which they pour, Twin Falls plunge 900' to join the Yoho River in Yoho National Park. Downstream, at Meeting of the Waters, the Yoho joins the Kicking Horse River which, together with the trans-Canada Highway and Canadian Pacific Railway, comes down from the pass which bears its name. It is of interest that the first reservation of what is now Yoho National Park was made in 1886 to preserve the beautiful scenery alongside the railroad, a beauty to which the numerous waterfalls largely contribute.

Les Chûtes de la Chaudière, Quebec, Canada Situated about five miles south-west of Quebec City, near Charny, Les Chûtes de la Chaudière lie on the La Chaudière River, which rises in the Notre Dame Mountains south of the St. Lawrence. The 100′ high falls, about two miles from the confluence of these two rivers, are one of the many attractions within easy reach of Quebec. They are in an area closely associated with early French exploration, fur-trading and missionary zeal; the site of a mission post for Abenaquis Indians was established near the falls in the early seventeenth century by Jesuit Fathers.

◀

Churchill Falls, Labrador, Canada Across the ice-scoured and lake-studded eastern extremity of the Canadian Shield flows the Churchill River. Over 600 miles long from its source in central Labrador to the Atlantic Ocean, in one sixteen mile stretch it descends 1000′, a drop which includes the 245′ Churchill Falls themselves. Higher than Niagara by some 60′, but rarely visited on account of the difficult terrain in which they lie, they nevertheless form the major source of hydro-electric power on this important river. At the point where the falls occur, the river bed suddenly narrows to a tenth of its former width, so that the immense weight of water is projected far forward beyond the brink of the precipice before falling into the granite ravine below. It is this constriction of the valley which explains the Indian name for the waterfall—'Patses-che-Wan' or 'the narrow place where the water descends'.

Montmorency Falls, Quebec, Canada   One of innumerable rivers draining from the Canadian Shield to the St. Lawrence valley, the Montmorency runs parallel to the Jacques Cartier River, named after the founder of Quebec, one of the earliest French settlements intended for fur trading in Canada. It is near Quebec that the Montmorency, originating in territory where countless lakes and streams aided the movements of trappers in birch-bark canoes, descends to the north bank of the St. Lawrence over 274' high falls. In 1885, a dam was built to provide Quebec City with electricity, and this severely restricted the water flow. The power facilitated the development of various industries, some of which were established soon after the city's foundation in 1608.

Aubrey Falls, Ontario, Canada Extending from Canada's Arctic shore southwards as far as the Great Lakes, most of the province of Ontario lies on the rocky, ice-worn Canadian Shield, with its myriad, interconnected shallow lakes. This is timber and fur country typified by innumerable waterfalls and rapids, particularly where the many rivers leave the Shield for the Great Lakes and St. Lawrence River. One such is the Mississagi, on which lie the 108′ high Aubrey Falls, near Thessalon. This exceptionally beautiful waterfall is sometimes likened to a miniature Niagara.

Kakabeka Falls, Ontario, Canada In an area where names such as Wild Goose, Grand Portage, Northern Light, Hunter Island, Sioux Lookout and Lac des Mille Lacs epitomise the historical geography of Ontario lie the Kakabeka Falls. They are situated on the trans-Canada Highway where, having left the shores of Lake Huron, it crosses the southern fringes of the Canadian Shield *en route* for Winnipeg. The river which here drops 128′ is the Kaministiquia, which means in Ojibway 'Thundering Waters'; it enters Lake Huron near Thunder Bay, opposite the Isle Royale National Park.

Rideau Falls, Ontario, Canada Three rivers meet in the heart of Ottawa in eastern Canada. Firstly, there is that which gave the Federal capital its name, a river born amid the lakes and forests of northern Ontario and stepping down to meet the great St. Lawrence in a series of rapids and waterfalls. In the city itself, for instance, there are the Deschênes Rapids, Remic Rapids and Chaudière Falls. At this point, the Ottawa is joined by two tributaries: from the north, the Gatineau drops from the Canadian Shield waterfall by waterfall; while from the south comes the canalised Rideau River. In the centre of Ottawa, only a short distance above the confluence, the latter drops over the scalloped rim of Rideau Falls in a folded and lace-like water curtain that is one of many attractions within the capital city.

Webster's Falls, Ontario, Canada Unlike the majority of Ontario's waterfalls, which lie amid the lakes and forests of the north, Webster's Falls are situated near the United States border some distance west of Niagara Falls. Their setting is the well-populated and prosperous farming country known as the Lake Peninsula, where the province's otherwise extreme climate is tempered by the presence of the Great Lakes. Resembling Tasmania's Russell Falls in their beautiful double cascade, they attract numerous visitors from the industrial cities close at hand.

Niagara Falls, Ontario, Canada One of the mightiest waterfalls in the world, Niagara is divided into the American Falls (on the left), 1000′ wide and 169′ high, and the Canadian Falls, 2950′ wide and 175′ high. Between them lies the international boundary and Goat Island, now reached by train to afford visitors a better vantage point. In addition, 'Maid of the Mist' sightseeing boats ply beneath the falls. During the winter, ice floes plunge over both falls to accumulate as massive icebergs in the frozen river below; moreover, all the surroundings scintillate beneath a fine covering of frozen spray, which also forms an icebridge at the American Falls.

Niagara Falls, Ontario, Canada Erosion along the crest of the Canadian (otherwise Horseshoe) Falls, seen here, is more rapid than that at the American Falls, although both are retreating towards Lake Erie at approximately four feet a year. This is because the former carries a much greater volume of water, a fact clearly demonstrated in 1848 when an ice blockage upstream caused the American Falls to run almost dry. The boat 'Maid of the Mist' customarily enters deep into the crescent of the Horseshoe Falls, where the weight of green water, falling from above with a deep and terrifying roar, seems almost to engulf its passengers.

Niagara Falls, New York State, U.S.A.   Despite the fact that both the Canadian and American Falls have been utilised for hydro-electric power with a resultant diminution in volume—and in the case of the former, in width also—they remain a natural wonder which attracts millions of visitors a year. As a night-time spectacle they are unmatched anywhere in the world. In the summer season the American Falls, seen here, are illuminated by twenty giant coloured floodlights, creating a magical atmosphere in which the crystal clear waters are transformed into a shimmering fantasy of ever changing colours. Photographed here by time exposure, the falls almost assume the fixed and unchanging aspect of sculpted marble.

Lower Mesa Falls, Idaho, U.S.A. Rising near Yellowstone National Park in Wyoming, Henry's Fork flows south to join the aptly named River Snake, tributary of the great Columbia River. In its upper course, the Snake drops over the Upper Mesa Falls (114′) and the Lower Mesa Falls (65′), seen here. Downstream the river enters the extensive Snake River Desert, a basaltic plateau through which, because snow-fed, it retains sufficient volume to carve a circuitous canyon.

American Falls and Shoshone Falls, Idaho, U.S.A. On its journey through the desert, the Snake River dr seaward over a succession of fine falls, including the Idaho (30′), American (50′), Twin (187′) and Shoshone (212′ addition, numerous underground springs emerge on the canyon sides and descend to join the main river. In this the Snake is dammed and diverted for irrigation purposes as well as for providing hydro-electric power. The Shosh Falls (above) plunge impressively over a horseshoe rim of basalt but are now greatly depleted by harnessing; American Falls (below) are named after a party of trappers who attempted the falls in canoes and suffered he casualties.

Snoqualmie Falls, Washington, U.S.A.
The Coast and Cascade Ranges of Washington's Pacific seaboard lie in the path of westerlies laden with rain after an uninterrupted journey over 4000 miles of ocean. Consequently the State is one of snowy mountains, rushing salmon rivers, numerous waterfalls, and tall timber. One of the four high routes over the Cascades is the Snoqualmie Pass, near which lie the 268′ high Snoqualmie Falls. Today they are utilised to provide electricity for nearby Seattle, Everett and Tacoma.

**Palouse Falls,
Washington, U.S.A.**
Rising in the Clearwater
Mountains of western
Montana, the Palouse
River enters the Snake
in south-eastern
Washington. Near the
confluence lie the
magnificent Palouse
Falls, one of the two
principal waterfalls in the
State, the other being
Snoqualmie. Plunging
vertically over the rim of
a vast rock amphitheatre,
they exemplify one aspect
of the fine scenery for
which Washington State
is noted.

Salt Creek Falls, Oregon, U.S.A. Lying beneath Diamond Peak in the snowy Cascades east of Eugene, Oregon, are the Salt Creek Falls. In an area noted for numerous waterfalls— Marion, Odin, Tumalo, Pringle, Paulina Creek, Steamboat, Toketee, Lemolo, South Umpqua— the 300′ high Salt Creek Falls stand supreme as the second highest in Oregon after Multnomah. It is a measure of their former remoteness that they were discovered only in 1887.

tnomah Falls and th Falls, Oregon, A. Dropping 620′ the rim of a volcanic , Multnomah Falls send clouds of y towards visitors in on's Columbia River e, east of Portland. s of trails lead to the r eleven waterfalls g this stretch of the South Falls (right) e of more than a n waterfalls in Silver State Park, a few s east of Salem. The passing behind the gives access to rs in the Park.

k Falls, Montana, **A.** Situated near er Two Medicine Lake e Glacier National of north-west tana, Trick Falls lie area of unspoiled forests carpeted moss and ferns. The ge phenomenon gives the falls their e is evident here; in spate the great ne of water plunging the upper rim eals a secondary ade emerging from a tone cave near the of the falls. With nset of the dry on, the upper fall ishes to reveal the, which apparently from a different, rranean source.

Tower Fall, Wyoming, **.S.A.** When travelling orth in Yellowstone ational Park beside the rand Canyon of the ellowstone towards Mammoth Hot Springs, he road approaches close the 2500′ deep ravine Tower Fall. Situated in tributary gulch in an rea of Douglas fir forest, e 132′ high fall can be pproached at close uarters by taking a otpath to its base. The ame is derived from the wer-like spires or innacles of rock which se hundreds of feet bove the brink of the ascade and guard Tower reek's approach to the rand Canyon.

Upper and Lower Yellowstone Falls, Wyoming, U.S.A.   Rising above Two Ocean Pass in the Absaroka Range of western Wyoming, the Yellowstone River is turned east by the Continental Divide, eventually to join the Missouri. Before leaving Wyoming, it enters Yellowstone National Park where, second in fame to the geysers, but second to none in spectacle, is the Grand Canyon of the Yellowstone. In this great ravine, which is not unlike the Colorado Canyon in the magnificence of its colours and architecture, are two tremendous waterfalls. At the 110′ high Upper Falls (above), the river at the rocky brink is turned backwards in a splendid arc of spray; half a mile below are the Lower Falls, 308′ high, twice the drop of the famed Niagara.

Nevada and Vernal Falls, California, U.S.A. One of the finest of the United States National Parks is that of Yosemite in the Sierra Nevada Range. The heart of the Park is the 3000' deep U-shaped Yosemite Valley, eroded out of granite by former glaciers and now drained by the beautiful Merced River on its way to the San Joaquin River and the Golden Gate at San Francisco. The river rises near Triple Divide Peak in the Sierra Nevada and, on entering the Yosemite Valley at its eastern end, negotiates two giant granite steps cut in its bed: the Nevada Fall (594'), named after its snowy whiteness and, half a mile downstream, the Vernal or Pivaak Falls (317'). The latter, Indian name means 'Cascade of Sparkling Water'.

Illilouette Fall, California, U.S.A. On its journey through the Yosemite Valley the pellucid, trout-filled waters of the Merced River receive numerous tributaries in the form of 'hanging' waterfalls from the ancient upland surface above. One of the first feeders to enter the main river in this way is Illilouette Creek, which rises on the southern boundary of the Yosemite National Park. It leaps 370′ from a hanging valley into a side gorge of the Merced Canyon below the Vernal Fall. Illilouette Fall is at its most beautiful in late Spring, when its white water curves like falling comets into surroundings bright with wild orange poppies.

Bridalveil Fall, California, U.S.A.
Before the placid Merced River leaves the level Yosemite Valley for its more turbulent descent beyond El Portal, it is joined by Bridalveil Creek which falls 620' from a glaciated canyon straight to the valley floor. The setting is magnificent: nearby lie the massive, granite Sentinel Rock and Cathedral Rocks; across the Merced, the sheer granite face of El Capitan towering to 7569'. Air currents caused by the Bridalveil's descent blow spray across, or even up the valley side like gossamer; they thus account not only for its popular name but for two others—Wawona, or 'The Wind in the Water' and Posono, 'The Spirit of Evil Winds', both given by the Yosemite Indians.

Yosemite Falls, California, U.S.A. Of the numerous 'hanging' waterfalls tributary to the Merced River, the most spectacular are Yosemite Falls. With an overall height of 2425', they rank as the second highest in the world after Angel Falls in Venezuela. Yosemite Creek, rising in the high Sierra, has a free fall of 1430' into the Yosemite Valley and then cascades over 675' towards the Merced, with another final straight drop of 320' in the Lower Fall. Being snow-fed, as are all the tributary creeks of the Merced within the Park, the waterfalls are at their best in May and June, when sightseers at close quarters are completely drenched by their spray. In late summer, on the other hand, they often dry up completely.

Ribbon Fall, California, U.S.A. One of the smallest of affluents serving to swell the Merced in the Yosemite National Park is Ribbon Creek, which rises behind El Capitan and enters the main valley almost opposite Bridalveil Creek. Ribbon Fall—sometimes called the Virgin's Tears—is well-named. From a point 3048′ above the Merced itself, the slender streamer of white water plunges without interruption for 1612′ towards the valley floor, making this the highest single fall in the area and placing it, in respect of height, in the same category as Upper Yosemite Fall (1430′) and Sutherland Falls, New Zealand (1904′).

Upper Waterwheel Fall, California, U.S.A. Within the Yosemite National Park but lying north of the much visited Yosemite Valley, i the remote Tuolumne River. It rises in Roosevelt Lake near Iny National Forest and, like the Merced, joins the San Joaquin River t enter the Pacific at San Francisco. In the Park, the river flows throug the so-called Grand Canyon of the Tuolumne—a granite-hewn ravin like the Yosemite Valley—where it has been dammed to form th Hetch-Hetchy Reservoir and supply San Francisco with water. Abov this Canyon lie the extraordinary Waterwheel Falls, where a swiftl sloping torrent on the river is interrupted by massive granite boulders which throw the water fifty feet or so into the air in gigantic arcs.

Opaaikaa Falls, Hawaii, U.S.A. Although one of the smallest of American states, the mid-Pacific islands of Hawaii possess a number of beautiful waterfalls, each enhanced by a setting of lush tropical vegetation. Opaaikaa Falls, on the garden island of Kauai, were named after a type of shrimp which the natives used to gather at one time from the rocks nearby.

**aka Falls, Hawaii,
.A.** Near the wet
tern coast of the main
nd of Hawaii itself, in
xotic, park-like
ing, lie the 420' high
ka Falls. They are
ated in a deep, green
e only a few miles
Hilo, the principal
.

**Rainbow Falls, Hawaii,
U.S.A.** Like Akaka Falls,
Rainbow Falls lie on one
of the small rivers which
radiate towards Hawaii's
north-eastern coast below
the lava fields and wide-
spreading volcanic cones
of Mauna Kea and Mauna
Loa. Draining from a
crater lake, the beautiful
twin falls are well-named,
since in the perpetual
Hawaiian sunshine their
waters are always
rainbow-hued. They have
their malevolent aspect,
however, in the legendary
monster which, dwelling
in the cave behind, is said
to emerge to devour all
who bathe there.

Blue Basin Cascade, Trinidad Where the Ande
cordilleras leave the South American mainland to fo
the curving archipelago of the West Indies, one sp
passes through Trinidad as three parallel mount
ranges. It is this topography, together with a wet su
equatorial climate, which give rise to a number of siza
waterfalls on this small island. In addition to the 300′ fa
of the Caura valley, for instance, and the Maraccas Fa
(340′), there is the exquisite Blue Basin Cascade in
valley of Diego Martin. This delicate, spun-glass water
enters a pool of azure blue and is the haunt of jewell
humming birds seeking the spray-cooled air.

Ocho Rios, Jamaica Set amid the green luxuriance of the north coast of tropical Jamaica is the Bay of Waterfalls, or Ocho Rios. As this Spanish name implies, as many as eight rivers here pour into the blue-green Caribbean along what is now one of the island's leading resort areas. Cascading through giant ferns, jacarandas and slender, feathered palms is one of the lesser known but most beautiful of these falls; more celebrated are the nearby Dunn's River Falls, which descend 600′ down a gradual rocky stairway of spray showers and refreshing pools—a favourite resort of bathers in the burning summer days.

Agoyan Falls, Ecuador In one of the most spectacular mountain landscapes in the world, the Avenue of Volcanoes in the Andes of Ecuador, the Pastaza River has its source. Leaving behind the snowy and majestic cones of Cotopaxi and Chimborazo which flank its head-waters, the little river starts eastwards on its long journey to join the Amazon. One of many such feeders from the Andes in this relatively unexplored part of the world, in its descent to the equatorial forests of Brazil it carves for itself a tremendous rocky valley in which lie the austere and solitary Agoyan Falls, 120′ high.

Laja Falls, Chile Otherwise known as the Niagara of Chile, the Laja Falls lie on a tributary of the Bio-Bio, which enters the sea near Concepcion. The Laja itself rises at a height of some 10,000′ on the slopes of the snow-capped volcano, Antuco, close to the Argentine frontier. It is a desolate region of high mountains between the difficult and little frequented Andean passes known as the Portillo de Chureo and the Paso Copahue. The 106′ high Laja Falls, in this savage setting, descend in a double cascade between precipitous walls of volcanic rock, their foaming whiteness in contrast to the sombre waters of the river itself, which is charged with a fine black débris.

Angel Falls, Venezuela In the Gran Sabana wilderness of south-east Venezuela is Canaima, an isolated area where lie the Angel Falls, highest in the world. Rising above the forests and savannahs of their lower slopes are several table mountains or 'tepuis', cliff-sided rock fortresses, one or even two miles high, whose tops lie permanently in the clouds and down whose rosy-red sides stream numerous slender falls of great height. This was the setting which inspired Conan Doyle's 'The Lost World'. Supreme in this land of mighty mountains and fabulous cascades is Auyan-tepuy, or Devil's Mountain, and its marvellous Salto Angel, the 3297′ high Angel Falls. They lie on the Carrao River, which feeds the Caroni, tributary of the Orinoco. As yet, they can only be properly seen from a plane and it was thus that they were first discovered in the 1930's by an American bush pilot, Johnny Angel—hence their name—who crash-landed his plane on Devil's Mountain.

Paulo Affonso Falls, Brazil One of the world's colossal falls, the little known Paulo Affonso lies on the mighty Rio Sao Fransisco in Brazil. This river rises not far from Rio de Janeiro on the Atlantic coast and journeys thence inland for nearly 2000 miles before entering the same ocean 1000 miles farther north. Not far from the river's mouth, the Paulo Affonso Falls descend first in a series of Upper Cascades (below), which pour 70′ into a tremendous basin named Mai da Cachoeira, the Mother of the Falls. It is from this boiling cauldron that the main fall (left), constricted to a width of only 60′, thunders 190′ or so into a canyon 800′ deep but barely 300′ wide. Paulo Affonso is one of the most stupendous, even terrifying of natural wonders, with the raging turmoil of the Upper Cascades, a spectacle unparalleled on any other river; the earth-shaking thunder of the main fall, and the foam and seething white water filling the lower canyon. In flood, the river may rise 40′ within this great ravine, while overflowing laterally to a width of ten miles.

Guayra Falls, Brazil   Draining virtually the whole of tropical south-eastern Brazil of the heavy trade wind rains which this plateau area attracts, are two of the world's great rivers, the Parana and the Rio Grande. These and their feeders descend towards the Rio de la Plata at Buenos Aires in a series of enormous steps, making this a region characterised by giant waterfalls. Supreme among them are, on the Rio Grande, the Saltos dos Patos e Maribondo; on the Parana, the Falls of Urubupunga and the Guayra Falls; and the Iguaçu Falls on an affluent of the Parana. Where volume is concerned, the Guayra Falls (or Sete Quedas) on the Parana are the greatest in the world. As the name implies however, the river here is divided into eighteen cataracts, one of which is seen here; they drop over a rocky rim over 5000 yards long into a deep, black ravine. In flood, when almost ten times as great as Niagara, the Guayra Falls inspire both awe and fear; on occasion their volume is such that they become one mammoth fall and the water in the gorge below rises no less than 50 yards.

75

Iguaçu Falls, Brazil 'After seeing Iguaçu Falls, it makes our Niagara Falls look like a kitchen faucet'. Thus did Eleanor Roosevelt describe the giant waterfall which lies at the meeting point of Brazil, Paraguay and Argentina. Audible fifteen miles away, the Iguaçu River here pours as twenty-one separate falls into a 250′ deep gorge. It occupies a width of three miles. In the rainy season, 140 million tons of water an hour make this descent, and on two occasions at least this flood water, dammed back by the swollen Parana downstream, has filled the gorge and obliterated the Iguaçu Falls altogether. The Union Fall (above), roaring into the Devil's Throat or Brazilian Pit, carries the main flow; for the very brave a peculiarity of the current allows a trip by small boat to within a few yards of the brink.

Kaieteur Falls, Guyana Like the Angel Falls, Kaieteur Falls lie on a river originating in the remote mountain wilderness where Venezuela and Guyana meet. This is the Potaro, confluent of the Essequibo, which passes through and diamond country to join the sea near Georgetown. In an area rich in waterfalls—King Edward VIII Fall and Ma Falls, for instance—lofty Kaieteur stands supreme and is unequalled in the world for its symmetry and majesty the cave behind the 822′ high curtain of water live the Kaieteur swallows, thousands of birds which continually in and out of the spray. Today, the falls are more accessible than formerly—periodically a small Grumman f boat brings sightseers from Georgetown, lands on the Potaro above the falls and takes off again over their brink.

Tequendama Falls, Colombia There are three high ranges of the Andes in Colombia, known as the Western, Central and Eastern Cordilleras. Between the two latter lies the valley of the great Magdalena River, which drains north to enter the Caribbean. Tributary to the Magdalena is the Bogota, flowing from the cool, healthy tablelands of the Eastern Cordillera; the river rises not far from Colombia's capital, also named Bogota, and it is here, twenty miles south-west of the city, that the 482′ high Tequendama Falls are to be found. Seen here during the dry summer months, the river drops serenely over the rim of its sandstone amphitheatre; in September, when in full spate, clouds of ascending spray obscure the splendour of the falls. Hidden too is the racing torrent in the canyon below, as well as the luxuriant tropical vegetation on its either side.

ASIA

Manavgat Falls, Turkey Forming a backdrop to the Mediterranean coast of Turkey is the southern barrier range of the high, dry Anatolian Plateau, the Taurus Mountains, which throw the winter rains southwards as numerous short rivers entering the Mediterranean Sea. Nearing the end of their journey near Side are the waters of Manavgat Falls, a beautiful spectacle as yet rarely visited in this lesser known part of Turkey.

Duden Falls, Turkey   The southern coast of Turkey is one of the most attractive in the Mediterranean, with its cliffs interspersed with magnificent beaches, its fishing villages, minarets, Crusader castles and citadels. Here, the Duden Falls (180′) descend the cliffs as numerous cataracts to enter the Gulf of Antalya near Lura beach.

ıvery Falls, India In peninsular India, where the great plateau or Deccan presents its high western edge—the
ıstern Ghats—to the wet summer monsoons off the Indian Ocean, the four principal rivers drain eastwards to the
 of Bengal. In flood, the volume of one of these, the Cauvery, is excelled only by the Khon Cataracts in Laos and
Brazilian Sete Quedas, making the Cauvery Falls, near Somnathpur in Mysore, one of the greatest falls in the world.
y are divided by the island of Sivasamudram into twin cascades, Gaganchukki, 'The Sky Spray' (300′), and Bara-
kki, 'The Heavy Spray' (182′). The setting is one of undulating jungle-clad highland, while in the gorge below lies
large Cauvery Falls electric power station serving the Kolar goldfields and the cities of Mysore and Bangalore.

Gokak Falls, India A second major river of Mysore draining eastwards is the Krishna, a tributary of which is the Ghataprabha. The
latter rises in the Western Ghats almost within sight of the Indian Ocean from which, during the advancing monsoon from June to
October, it receives torrential rains. Only 100 miles from its source, where the Gokak Falls lie, it is already of sufficient volume to ensure
that these, although only 170′ high, are one of the major falls of Asia. When in full spate the water, rust red and charged with débris,
pours with such force over a sandstone precipice as to be completely hidden by a mass of golden spray, while the rapids above the fall
are a turmoil of raging waters.

Khon Cataracts, Laos Flowing side by side in deep and narrow ravines carved between 20,000' high mountain peaks, three of the world's greatest rivers make their way southwards through the high ranges which encircle the Tibetan plateau. These three are the Mekong, Salween and Yangtze-Kiang. The first of these enters the South China Sea through an extensive delta in South Vietnam but the whole of its middle course lies in Laos, where the Khon Cataracts are situated. Like the Sete Quedas of Brazil, they are not waterfalls in the generally accepted sense of the word, but on account of their tremendous width of over 14,000 yards and their great volume, they merit inclusion among the giant falls of the world. When in full flood in September the mighty Mekong, stained red from the sandstone gorges of its upper tract, and struggling through the innumerable forested islands which here impede its progress, is an amazing spectacle.

soppa Falls, India These are situated in Mysore on the River Sharavathi which rises in the Western Ghats and flows only 100 miles re reaching the Indian Ocean near Honavar. During the summer monsoon season, when rain falls here at the rate of many inches y, the falls can be located only by their thunder and the clouds of spray which obscure them. Dropping 829' into a chasm almost ' deep, they are at this season one of the greatest natural wonders of the world. At low water, the falls naturally divide into four arate cataracts, seen above; they are named the Raja, Roarer, Rocket and Rani. Nearby is the giant hydro-electric power station ch produces the bulk of electricity in Mysore.

83

Chamarel Falls and Rochester Falls, Mauritius Five hundred miles east of Malagasy in the Indian Ocean lies Mauritius, a mountainous island enjoying a sub-tropical climate with high humidity and heavy rainfall. Of the numerous waterfalls on Mauritius the second highest after the virtually inaccessible Tamarind Falls (960'), are the 320' high Chamarel Falls (left). They lie on the Rivière du Cap in the Savane Mountains. The pretty Rochester Falls (right) on the river of the same name are situated close to the seaside village of Souilla, on the south coast.

Diamamou Falls and Rivière du Poste Falls, Mauritius The falls of Mauritius are shown to best advantage when in spate amid the lush green vegetation of the wet season. The Diamamou Falls (below) occur where the Grand River South-East drops 63′ over a high basalt precipice set amid dense forest. Flowing also to the east coast, the Rivière du Poste plunges 56′ in the falls to which it gives its name.

Pagsanjan Falls, Philippines
One of the most exciting journeys to be made in the Philippines is that by river from Manila, on the island of Luzon, through dense jungle and deep canyons to see the Pagsanjan Falls. The trip is made by 'banca', paddled by two boatmen up the wild rapids which lie below the falls. Struggling between 300′ high cliffs covered with palms, begonias and orchids, the small boat passes nineteen smaller cascades before Pagsanjan Falls, with their enormous under-cliff cave, are reached. The return journey with the strong current is even more exciting.

ria Cristina Falls, ilippines Distant about miles from the south-east st of mainland Asia lies the up of over 7000 islands ed the Philippines. The ond largest of these is danao where, just a few es inland from Iligan City ts north coast, the Maria stina Falls are situated. This ne highest waterfall in the ilippines, as well as the most utiful. Despite the fact that now a source of power industrial plants in the area, s helping to diversify a dominantly agricultural nomy, its loveliness ains unimpaired.

AUSTRALASIA

Millstream Falls, Queensland, Australia   From the Darling Downs near Brisbane to the lofty Atherton Tableland behind Cairns, the Eastern Highlands or Great Dividing Range in Queensland lie in the path of the wet south-east Trade winds and are alive with waterfalls. Among the widest in Australia, Millstream Falls lie on the Atherton Tableland amid the tropical rain forests of the north.

Wallaman Falls, Queensland, Australia Possibly the most impressive of Australian waterfalls are those which give their name to the Wallaman National Park. This lies, along with many other Parks, in the forests of the Great Dividing Range overlooking the tropical cane and cattle lands of coastal Queensland. Seen here at low water, the falls divide into an upper and a lower cataract; in flood, when a rainbow-fringed cloud of spray obscures their base, the water drops in a single free fall of 1000′, making this one of the world's highest falls.

Millaa Millaa Falls, Queensland, Australia Not far distant from the Millstream Falls in the lush, green mountain forest of north Queensland are the Millaa Millaa Falls. Dropping straight and sheer into the still, dark pool of their own making, they rival the Kaieteur Falls of Guyana in their symmetry and beauty, if not their height.

Barron Falls, Queensland, Australia
Considered to be at one time the most majestic in Australia, the Barron Falls, named after the river on which they lie, now retain little of their former glory owing to their utilisation for hydro-electric power. Nevertheless, at certain times, for the benefit of tourists using the marvellously scenic Cairns-Kuranda railway, water is released to roar down more than 1000′ of cataracts into the rocky ravine below. It is only then that their considerable volume, derived from continual heavy rains on the Great Divide, can be fully enjoyed.

Katoomba Falls, Fitzroy Falls and Ebor Falls, New South Wales, Australia In New South Wales where the Great Dividing Range reaches its maximum height lie many of the continent's finest falls. There are, for instance, the 1580' Wollomombi Falls, which drop into a gloomy ravine in the New England Range near Armidale, and the lofty Minnamurra Falls, south of Sydney, which lie hidden in a dark and cleft-like chasm. Not far from these lie the spectacular Katoomba Falls (top left), where the river of that name, high in the Blue Mountains behind Sydney, makes two uninterrupted leaps, separated by a series of rocky ledges, in all a drop of 540'. To the south, nearer Canberra, are the Fitzroy Falls (top right), where the Yarrunga Creek leaps first 400', then a further 200', to join the Shoalhaven River. In the north of the State, not far from the Wollomombi Falls, the Ebor Falls (bottom left), drop 500' over a series of three horse-shoe shaped tiers.

Russell Falls, Tasmania, Australia One of numerous striking waterfalls in this mountainous island lying in the track of the moisture-laden 'Roaring Forties', the Russell Falls are situated near the entrance to the Mount Field National Park, some 50 miles from Hobart. The falls are about 120′ high overall and consist of two vertical drops only a few yards apart. They lie on the Russell River, one of several draining the south-east corner of the Mawson Plateau, the principal feature of the National Park.

Rouna Falls, Papua New Guinea A series of half-submerged fold mountain ranges, the islands which lie athwart the Equator north of Australia provide the rugged and rain drenched setting for countless rivers of short and rapid descent. On Papua New Guinea, the 250′ high Rouna Falls of the Laroki River (above) are situated on the Sogeri Plateau near Port Moresby; they are a magnificent sight in the rainy season from November to February, when the cataracts above and below the falls are a seething mass of white water. The Rouna Falls are sufficiently remote not to have been discovered by white man until a century ago but even more inaccessible is the waterfall (below) in the Talasea area east of the Toriu River, Papua New Guinea. Buried in impenetrable equatorial jungle, its beauty escapes virtually all eyes but those of the aerial photographer and in that respect compares with the Angel Falls, Venezuela.

Bowen Falls, New Zealand Like those of the Norwegian coast, the ice-carved fjords or sounds of south-west New Zealand are enhanced by the waterfalls of many hanging valleys. The most impressive of these are the 504′ high Bowen Falls on Milford Sound, South Island. When in full spate with meltwater from the Barren Ranges of the Southern Alps, the falls are impeded by a tremendous rock barrier in their path. This throws their waters skywards in a widely curving arc that resembles a colossal fire hydrant at work—one of the most magnificent sights in the country.

Sutherland Falls, New Zealand Situated not far distant from Bowen Falls in the rain-drenched area known as 'Fiordland' are the Sutherland Falls, the Arthur River on which they lie entering the head of Milford Sound. In three elegant, free-falling cascades they descend from rock basin to rock basin in a total drop of 1904', being not dissimilar to Yosemite Falls in California both in height and appearance. Like the latter they are also the highest fall in their own continent and are at their finest in late spring when swollen with icy waters from the snowfields which feed them.

Huka Falls, New Zealand While the fiord coast of south-west New Zealand is the most scenic area in South Island, it is the volcanic area around Lake Taupo which attracts sightseers in North Island. Where the mighty force of the Waikato River leaves this lake, it shoots through a steep-sided ravine only 30′ wide to produce the Huka Falls which, although of no great height, have the greatest volume of any in New Zealand. These waters of the Waikato, traversing an area of continual subterranean activity in the form of hot springs, mud volcanoes and minor earth tremors, are so disturbed that they were long thought by the Maoris to be inhabited by fabulous monsters.

Tiavi Falls, Western Samoa The islands of Western Samoa, situated in the South Pacific almost two thousand miles from New Zealand, enjoy a marine tropical climate which gives rise to a luxuriant forest vegetation. This is particularly so in the mountainous island of Upolo, most fertile of the group. Tiavi Falls plummet 600′ into the intense green of the Samoan jungle, glittering as they fall. They lie a short distance from Apia on Upolo and are seen here from a scenic look-out point.

Victoria Falls, Rhodesia One of Africa's largest rivers, the Zambesi rises in western Zambia, afterwards flowing southwards to the border with Rhodesia, where lie the Victoria Falls. Considered by many to be the most spectacular of their kind in the world, they also have the native name of 'Mosi-o-Tunya', or 'The Smoke that Thunders'. It was this 'smoke' or rising vapour, ascending from the five main falls in the well-known 'five fingers' that, from a distance of twenty miles, first attracted David Livingstone's attention over a century ago. One mile wide at this point, the Zambesi serenely approaches the immense drop of 355′ which lies ahead, finding its way smoothly through numerous islands. So quietly does the current flow that at low water it is possible to bathe in pools near the brink of the falls and to wade across the river. In addition, from the Zambian side a launch cruises out daily on a 'camera safari', and from the Rhodesian, a 'Zambesi Sky Safari'.

...toria Falls, Rhodesia In
...il and May, floodwaters
...the upper Zambesi reach
...falls, which at this season
...ome an almost unbroken
...ain of water a mile in
...th. Dropping into a fear-
...e, black basalt gorge barely
...yards wide, the river turns
...ght angles to race towards
...end of this ravine, where
...the only exit. There it pours
...a second narrow defile
...wn as the Boiling Pot,
...ch in turn leads to the 40
...-long zig-zag canyon
...ugh which the river has
...ed its way, making six
...her gorges. At low water
...river finds its way over the
...k of the falls in many
...arate cataracts, most
...utiful of which are the
...bow Falls in the centre.
...y are named after the
...dreds of rainbows which
...n and fade about them,
...ough any spectator standing
...in the spray from the falls
...also find himself enclosed
...in a small rainbow,
...rcling him like a hoop.

Victoria Falls, Zambia The opposite rim of the canyon from that over which the Zambesi plunges offers spectacular head-on view of the falls over almost their whole width, from the Eastern Cataracts in Zambia (seen here), past the Rainbow Falls, Horseshoe Fall and Main Falls, to the Devil's Cataract in Rhodesia beside Dr. Livingstone's statue (seen overleaf). When in flood, 60 million gallons o water per minute crash into the gorge, with a deafening sound like thunder. Dangerous winds strong enough to blow a man over ar generated and whirlwinds of blinding spray drench the onlooker, obliterating the falls from view. It is the constantly rising and driftin vapour that produces the so-called Rain Forest—a dense, dripping jungle of brilliant green—which surrounds the falls and contrast markedly with the parched Zambian bush in which they lie. This same spray shrouds trains passing over the bridge which crosses th second gorge at a height of 310' above the river, and carries the Cape-Cairo Railway.

Luando Falls and Duke of Braganza Cataract, Angola

Lying along the fringes of Africa's selva or tropical rain forest, northern Angola in the wet season is a land of innumerable waterfalls. The majority are remotely situated and lie principally on feeders of the Zaire (Congo) or the Cuanza River, which reaches the Atlantic near Luanda, 300 miles south of the Zaire estuary. The Luando Falls (above) drop 220′ over a hundred yard wide precipice into a forested ravine before eventually their waters meet the Cuanza south of Malanje. To their north, on another confluent of this same river, lies the powerful Duke of Braganza Cataract or Quedas Duque de Bragança (below). Here the Lucala, which joins the Cuanza downstream from the Luando, makes a glorious display as it curves over a 100′ wide rock rim into a wilderness of orange trees, bananas, palms and giant ferns.

Rua Cana Falls, Angola
Situated in a little known region of Africa are the Rua Cana Falls on the Cunene River, which forms the boundary between Angola and Namibia (formerly South-West Africa). Rising not far from the Cuanza River in Angola's central highlands, the Cunene, like most African rivers, must negotiate the descent from the African plateau to the sea. This it achieves some 200 miles from the Atlantic in a series of cascades, rapids and waterfalls, the largest group of which are the 406′ high Rua Cana Falls. In the dry season, their various slender channels of water seem appropriate to the semi-arid landscape in which they lie; in spate, however, these cascades unite to become one vast curtain of water almost half a mile wide and rank as one of the greatest waterfalls in the world.

Kabalega Falls, Uganda The largest of African rivers, the Nile receives a great proportion of the water which sustains it across the desert in Egypt from lakes in the African Rift Valley and from Lake Victoria on the East African Plateau. Within a few miles of the Equator and fed by heavy rains, the Victoria Nile emerges from the lake which shares its name and flows northwards to drop into Lake Albert in the Rift Valley. Here its crocodile-infested waters surge 400′ downwards over the Kabalega (formerly Murchison) Falls, first confined in a narrow 25′ chasm, then exploding into a 130′ fall into the valley below before resuming their calmer journey across half the African continent towards a more temperate Mediterranean Sea.

Tisisat Falls, Ethiopia Whereas the White Nile, which has its beginnings in Lake Victoria, contributes the main volume of water to the Lower Nile of Egypt from October to July, this role is taken over during the summer months by another principal feeder. This is the Blue Nile, issuing from the Highlands of Ethiopia. Originating in Lake Tana, within twenty miles this last-named tributary pours over a 200' high precipice into a deep and narrow gorge. These are the 400 yard wide Tisisat Falls, seen here in spate as the waters of the Blue Nile hurry down to their meeting with the White Nile at Khartoum, in the Sudan.

Maletsunyane Falls, Lesotho The Drakensberg Range is the spine of South Africa and nowhere is it more spectacular than on the border between Natal and Lesotho, where the peaks rise to 10,000' or more. There, on the 10,200' Mont aux Sources, highest peak in the Republic, rises the Orange River. It crosses Lesotho, the roof-top state of South Africa, before beginning its slow descent across the African plateau towards the Atlantic Ocean. One of the principal tributaries of the Orange is the Maletsunyane which originates beneath the 10,158' peak Thaba Putsoa. Dropping 660' in a single leap at the Maletsunyane Falls, the river plunges into a grim and rocky cauldron, a place held much in fear by the Basutos.

Kogun Falls, Nigeria Tributary of the Niger, third largest river in Africa, the Kafanchan rises in the open woodland and savannah which clothe the hot, dry central plateau of northern Nigeria. On this river are the Kogun Falls, noted for the deep caves which lie beneath their brink. In the summer rainy season, from April to October, when Kafanchan races in spate to join the Niger and so on towards the mangrove swamps of Nigeria's humid coast, the falls are a splendid sight.

Manchewe Falls, Malawi The country of Malawi comprises little more than the southern extremity of the narrow African Rift Valley and its faulted western slopes. Draining from the latter towards Lake Malawi (Nyasa), which here occupies the valley floor, are the Manchewe Falls, cascading step by step through the lush vegetation of the Livingstonia Escarpment to enter the western side of the lake near Florence Bay.

Montrose Falls, Transvaal, Republic of South Africa Not far from the source of the winding Crocodile River, tributary of the Limpopo, where it begins life on the magnificent escarpment of the Drakensberg Mountains, lie the 180′ high Montrose Falls. They are situated in Schoeman's Kloof, a lush and beautiful valley leading from the grassy and temperate Highveld to the sub-tropical Lowveld. Along this valley, curving with the meanderings of the river, runs the main road from Johannesburg to the Kruger National Park; it crosses the Crocodile just above the falls.

Lone Creek Falls, Transvaal, Republic of South Africa The Lone Creek Falls, on a river named Lone Creek by early gold prospectors, plunge about 230′ over a volcanic cliff into a deep pool protected as a breeding place for trout. They are situated in a forestry reserve on a terrace of the Drakensberg, an area which has many striking waterfalls. Among them are the Bridal Veil, Horseshoe, Forest, Berlin, Lisbon and Sabie Falls, as well as the lofty Graskop Falls, difficult of access, and the twin Mac Mac Falls, so named after Scots prospectors.

Howick Falls, Natal, Republic of South Africa Among the most splendid of South Africa's waterfalls are the 280′ high Howick Falls on the Umgeni River. They and the nearby town of Howick are named after the Northumberland home of Earl Grey, a former British Colonial Secretary. The falls are situated in the beautiful rolling countryside of the Natal Midlands, across which the Umgeni, from its source in the Drakensberg near the borders of Lesotho, makes its way to reach the Indian Ocean immediately north of Durban.

Aughrabies Falls, Cape Province Republic of South Africa Rising on the famous Mont aux Sources in the High Drakensberg behind South Africa's east coast, the Orange River journeys thence westwards to the South Atlantic. So great is its volume that, as it crosses a progressively more arid continent in the rain shadow of the Drakensberg, it is able to maintain its course across the Kalahari Desert. It is here, in a wilderness of bare rock, salt pans, acacias and thorny shrubs that the river, a thundering torrent of brown and amber, pours into a six mile-long rock chasm 600′ below the desert surface. This is Aughrabies, one of the mammoth waterfalls of the world, so inaccessible it can only be satisfactorily photographed from the air. The alien setting of impassable ravines among which it lies; the heat and desolation; the gloomy, sullen canyon where lives the monstrous, all-devouring 'Groote Slang' of Hottentot imagination—all these place Aughrabies apart among the world's waterfalls; if it is beautiful at all, its beauty is of a very different kind. In the still and silent desert its roar and tumult, even at a time of low water, fills the observer with fear. In spate, when the raging waters rise high in the canyon, Aughrabies cannot be approached at all; a cloud of spray and a distant thunder then indicate its presence over a radius of 40 miles.

INDEX